Living with Grandpa Joseph

by Joe Adair
illustrated by Dan Grant

Scott Foresman
is an imprint of

Glenview, Illinois • Boston, Massachusetts • Chandler, Arizona
Upper Saddle River, New Jersey

TABLE OF CONTENTS

Chapter 1
The News About Grandpa

It was a cool fall day in Denver, Colorado. Mom parked her car in front of the house. Her twins, Kevin and Annie, jumped out to race to the door. They were ten-years-old. They were not identical twins, but they did share a strong resemblance to one another.

As soon as Mom opened the door, they all made a dash to answer the ringing phone. "Hello," Annie said breathlessly.

"Annie, get Mom," said Dad's voice on the phone. Annie saw a lurking fear in Mom's eyes as she took the receiver from Annie.

"Katie, I have some bad news. I am at the hospital with your father. He slipped in the shower and broke his hip. Come quickly."

Mom and the children rushed to the hospital.

They all shared a memory of Grandpa Joseph. He was 82 years old and had lived alone since his wife died three years earlier.

"I hope Grandpa is okay," Kevin said softly from the back seat. The children loved their grandfather.

They quickly found Grandpa's room. As soon as Grandpa saw them all, he smiled. "I will be fine in no time."

The doctor had a different idea. He turned to the children's parents and said, "Your father's hip will take time to heal. He should not live alone."

At home that night, Mom asked the children, "How would you feel about Grandpa living with us?"

"That would be great!" cried Kevin. The children loved the stories he told about being a colonel in World War II.

Chapter 2
Grandpa Moves In

The next morning, Kevin and Annie helped their parents get the computer room ready for Grandpa Joseph. When their parents were busy, Annie said quietly to Kevin, "How are we going to watch TV or have computer time?"

"I know," Kevin whispered back. "Probably never."

"Hey, Mom," Annie blurted out, "don't give away all our space. It's not fair!"

"I'm sorry, but this is the only room we can spare. We're all going to have to adjust," Mom said.

"Besides, this room affords Grandpa a great view of the Rocky Mountains. You know how he loves to paint them. Don't worry, Annie, it will only be for a little while."

The family drove to the hospital to pick up Grandpa. When they arrived, he was waiting outside in a wheelchair. Annie noticed he didn't look very happy. When they took him to his own home to pick up his clothes, a photo album, and his painting supplies, Annie asked, "Grandpa, what's wrong?"

"It's not easy for me to leave my home," he replied softly.

Grandpa Joseph sat quietly as all the family unpacked his things in his new room. He looked at all his belongings stacked in piles on the floor around him.

"Katie, thank you for taking care of me. I hope that I'm not making too much trouble for you and the kids," Grandpa said.

"Dad, we are so happy to have you here with us," Mom smiled back at him. "Please don't feel like you are any trouble at all. Even Annie and Kevin will get used to giving up some time on the computer."

After all the boxes were moved in and unpacked, Grandpa Joseph sat over by the window. He stared out at the beautiful mountains in the distance.

"Dad, what's wrong?" Mom asked.

"I can't drive my car. I can't stand in the kitchen and cook for myself. I can't even ride to the park and paint," said Grandpa.

"Things will get better," Mom said. She wondered to herself, though, if that was true.

Just then she noticed his large brown box of paints at the closet door. She took it out and placed it on the table in front of him.

"Dad, you can still paint," Mom said. "You have your favorite mountains right there in the window. Just rest for now. This has been a busy day."

Chapter 3
The Children Talk with Grandpa

"Grandpa, are you awake?" Kevin asked as he led Annie into the room.

"Yes, I am awake. I was just taking a little nap. I'm glad to see you two. Come in."

Grandpa moved from his bed to his wheelchair.

"Would you kids like to hear another story about when I was young and in the army?" The children nodded and sat on the couch near his chair.

"All right, did I ever tell you about the time I was trapped behind enemy lines with secret plans for the war?"

"Grandpa, you never told us that story," Kevin said. "Start from the beginning and tell us the whole story!"

Grandpa Joseph smiled and leaned forward in his chair.

The children loved how Grandpa's forehead wrinkled when he came to scary parts. They knew he was a hero in the war, but Grandpa never really said he was. As he told the story, Annie sat at his feet to hear better.

Mom was making dinner in the kitchen and heard her father telling another story. She called to Dad, and they both went to listen as well. Now everyone was sitting and listening to Grandpa Joseph tell his story. Looking down at his family gathered around him, Grandpa smiled. Mom was happy to see the old glint in his eye again.

When Grandpa Joseph finished, everyone clapped. "Now," Annie said, "tell us how you met Grandma!"

Grandpa Joseph smiled. "We met during the war. She was a nurse. We bought a house right here in Denver. She was such a beautiful and kind woman. You know, Annie, you have a resemblance to your grandmother."

Annie blushed.

Kevin noticed Grandpa's photo albums. "Can we look through these?" he asked.

"I'd love to share these with you," said Grandpa. "Let's start with this one. This is your family history too." He opened up a big blue book and pointed at the photos.

"This is me when I was your age, Kevin," he said. "I lived in this quaint old house here." Grandpa Joseph turned the pages of the old album, which were colored in pale brown and pink palettes.

"Annie, come here," Grandpa said. "This is a picture of your grandmother." Annie and her mother went closer to see it.

"Wow! Annie does look a lot like her," Mom said.

Chapter 4
Grandpa Helps Out

The next day, Grandpa tried to help out at dinner. From his wheelchair, he beat eggs in a bowl. The bowl fell out of his hands and onto the floor. "No problem!" said Mom, but she could see how upset her father was.

When the children came home from school, Grandpa was sleeping. "Shhh," said Mom. "You must be quiet."

"Great," said Kevin. "I wanted to practice my recorder and now I can't!" He was very upset.

Grandpa Joseph had heard the children. "Annie! Kevin!" he called. "Come here for a minute!" The children slowly walked to his room.

Grandpa was smiling. "You know," he said, "I'd love to hear some recorder music." Kevin's grin widened. He started to play.

"I was thinking, too," said Grandpa to Annie, "how much I'd love to paint a picture with you. Would you like that?"

Annie's face brightened. "Would I!" she said.

On another day not long after, Mom went into Grandpa's room and saw how sad he was. "Are you all right?" she asked.

"I am sorry for causing you so much trouble. You do so much for me, and I feel I am not doing anything," Grandpa said.

"That's not true, Dad! Annie is painting now because of you. And Kevin is actually practicing more because he gets to play for you when he does!"

Grandpa Joseph smiled.

"Soon, you will be well enough to go home," Mom said. "And guess what? We will really miss you!"

That afternoon, when Kevin and Annie came home, they ran outside to play ball.

"Could I go outside too?" Grandpa asked. "Would you help wheel me to the backyard, Katie?"

Grandpa Joseph loved watching his grandchildren laugh and play together in the yard. "Catch!" said Annie, gently throwing him a ball.

The next morning Grandpa Joseph watched the sun rise over the Rocky Mountains. It was beautiful to see the orange, red, and yellow colors in the sky.

"I feel like painting today!" Grandpa said.

"The Rockies?" Mom asked. That's your favorite subject."

"Not anymore!" said Grandpa. "Would you please hand me my palette? I want to paint something more precious. I'm going to paint all of you!"

Seniors Reach Amazing Goals

Many senior citizens make headlines for amazing achievements. Bill Hagman, who is over sixty, is an inspiration to seniors and kids. He started running after he turned fifty years old. To date, he has run eleven marathons.

Other seniors like downhill skiing. Called *"silver streakers"* or "seniors heading downhill," these senior skiers number almost seven million. One skier, at eighty-one years of age, skis 150 days each season, and many others travel all over the United States and Europe to ski.

Other seniors enjoy making life a little better in their cities or neighborhoods. Some provide recreation for teens, with tutoring and trips. Others lead recycling efforts. Still others help the Red Cross enlist volunteers to deliver meals or to give blood. These seniors receive awards as citizens who make a difference.